How to Secure Your Smartphone and Mobile Devices

William G. Perry, Ph.D.

Liability Disclaimer

Dedication

This book is dedicated to Robert J. Glick, a patriot, brave solider, law enforcement officer and loyal friend. You enriched the lives of everyone who knew you. Rest in peace my friend. You are sorely missed. *Brother Bill*

Table of Contents

How to Secure Your Smartphone and Mobile Devices

Security controls have not kept pace with the risks posed by mobile devices. Entrepreneurs are under pressure to accept the risks due to several factors, such as anticipated cost savings and employee demand for more convenience sometimes without the ability to (deploy) defensive mitigations - - NIST

Introduction

The use of mobile devices has exploded. The "mobile genie" is out of the bottle and its use is expanding dramatically. The rate of growth is phenomenal. Sources suggest that it's as high as thirty percent (30%) annually. Handheld computers of all types are becoming more powerful and cheaper.

Mobile computing devices include laptops, tablets, notepads, smartphones, computer watches and even digital computing nodes.

'On the go' computing has changed the way business is done and the way people communicate. Mission critical information, even including video, can now be sent anywhere on the planet where connectivity is possible. Compounding the security challenge is the fact that today's portable computing equipment is just as powerful as desktop computers.

People who use the Internet to conduct business can literally be out of the office and have the ability to routinely access information from virtually anywhere. Old information security boundaries have disappeared. There are serious downsides of mobile computing about which users should be aware.

The negatives include major **risks** related to maintaining the confidentiality, availability and integrity of information. More than two million versions of malware are in existence. One report by IDG indicated that seventy-four percent (74%) of respondents reported their organizations have experienced a data breach as the result of weak mobile security. Mobile computing devices are now capable of storing more information and they are able to access large databases.

Smartphones, for example, aren't protected by specialized firewalls that can block attacks. Securing personal communication and sensitive business data in a mobile environment presents unique and significant challenges. Cybercriminals are aware and they are increasingly targeting smartphones.

Cybersecurity risks include many of the same threats associated with desktops, network computing and more. WiFi access points are vulnerable eavesdropping spots. Hackers and crackers can gain access to your personal communication devices and install malware on your home and business computers.

You can strengthen the security of your smartphone, tablet or other portable computing devices by following the suggestions in this publication.

Mobile Computing Operating Systems and Platforms

There are two *main* operating systems for smartphones and operating systems in use (iOS and Android). The iOS is published by Apple.

Apple makes the iPhone and iPad and other portable laptops.

A number of hardware manufacturers run the Android operating system. Among the hardware manufacturers are Nokia, Samsung, Google and others. The publisher of the Android operating system is Google.

There are far more Android-based phones than Apple phones in use.

Threats and Vulnerabilities

Both iOS and Adroid have vulnerabilities and face threats. Remember, however, that the number of Android devices significantly outnumbers Apple's installed user base.

iOS apps are vetted by Apple's iTunes. Apple's iOS operating system is far less vulnerable to malware attacks as well as various threats than the Android OS. iPhones, however, aren't immune from cybercrime. The number of vulnerabilities associated with the iOS is on the rise.

Google Play distributes Android apps but it's generally believed that the security standards for apps that run on Android are lower than those distributed by iTunes for the iPhone

Users should understand that there is a difference between threats and vulnerabilities. Each is unique. A threat (e.g. a cyber criminal) exploits vulnerabilities (e.g. a failure to use a password). A risk occurs when a threat and vulnerability intersect.

Even legitimate apps that are downloaded can leak information. Your device contains a number of identifiers, your location, personal contacts and IMEI number as a MAC address.

Threats

Threats are hazards faced by your information assets. A cybercriminal who is actively trying to crack into your smartphone is an example of a threat. Recently reports in Security Magazine have exposed the fact that even some developer tools have been shown to infect apps. One example of a threat could be rising flood water outside of your home.

A smartphone or tablet user can reduce security risks by becoming aware of security best practices, forethought and caution. Below are a number of specific threats against mobile devices.

Social Engineering – An attack method that can be used by cybercriminals to make the device owner behave in a manner that serves the interests of the attacker. One example of a social engineering attack might be to send the mobile device owner a message that tricks the user to click on a malware site. A malicious software package could then be installed on the user's smart device and exploited. One threat is ransomware, which is an exploit that seizes control of the mobile device. The cybercriminal only releases it when the victim pays a ransom.

Mobile device users should avoid opening or responding to text messages from unknown sources. Be cautious about opening messages that appear to be from banks, loan companies or credit card companies.

Shoulder Surfers – People who wish to eavesdrop on you and your confidential data could easily see you entering your password into a mobile device. Users should be on guard against people who might directly observe a user or engage in "shoulder surfing". It can be used to acquire personal identification numbers (PIN), login credentials (e.g. password, etc.), and other confidential information.

Stealing sensitive information from electronic devices is particularly effective in crowded places (reception areas, airports and business centers) because it is relatively easy to "innocently" get close to people using devices. Consider how easy it would be, with today's mobile phones, to snap high-resolution pictures or to record videos for playback. Cybercriminals can steal additional information from shoulder surfing such as:
   a. personal data being entered into a form
   b. the entering of a personal PIN at an automated teller machine or a POS data terminal

c. passwords at a cyber cafe, public and university libraries, or airport kiosks
d. a code for a rented locker in a public place where you might store your mobiles devices.
e. credit card information on your hand-held tablet or phone while the person in line next to you shoots video from his phone

Public WiFi Spaces – Wireless access point networks facilitate the compromise of tablets, smartphones and laptops. Extreme caution should be exercised when using a public WiFi site. Avoid accessing and working upon critical software and data in publicly accessible sites. Broadcast signals can be "listened to" or stolen. You should avoid transmitting confidential information to and from public networks.

Nefarious individuals can and will intercept any information that you send over a public Wi-Fi space. Users should deploy the highest level of encryption when working in a public WiFi space. You might want to consider using a VPN (Virtual Private Network). Cybercriminals would find it very difficult and resource intensive to successfully "hack" a VPN. It's likened to an electronic tunnel, which is very difficult to access.

Public WiFi spaces represent a variety of other threats.

Cybercriminals can, for example, buy and use a hardware device that mimics a WiFi hotspot. The equipment can receive a wireless signal(s), capture wireless traffic, store "key log" password entries, and generally gain a perspective on what is being transmitted by anyone who is targeted within range.

The Pineapple, a WiFi cracking device, is even capable of reversing SSH (Secure SHell) encryption. You can watch videos on YouTube™ that illustrates the "take over" of private WiFi traffic.

Misconfigured WiFi Networks – Misconfigured networks can leave your mobile device open without your knowledge. A network that is improperly installed can "pretend" your communications are secure when they aren't. An unsuspecting wireless device user on a misconfigured network is at serious risk of losing his private and confidential information.

Another example might be a wireless access point(s) in a hotel. Each access point could be a different brand or configured in a haphazard manner. Each could theoretically pose its own unique threats. Even with a secure VPN connection a misconfigured network could make it possible for an attacker to 'punch through' and gain open access from either side of the connection (including the corporate network).

The phrase "misconfigured network" could just as easily be read as meaning "unpatched network". A vulnerable network device without a current patch is equal to a misconfigured network and can leave connections open to nefarious attacks. Users should regularly install software patches that are distributed by legitimate manufacturers and publishers.

SMS Attacks – SMS, also known as "texting," can be used to launch a malware attack. One SMS attack method, associated with the Android operating system, can deliver very dangerous and invasive malware attacks. Such threats, if enabled, can be used to gain access to user names, passwords and other confidential information.

Some SMS attacks originate from a legitimate source such as your bank. Cybercriminals that masquerade as genuine businesses can be made to create a command and control server on the user's device. They can literally gain control of the unsuspecting user's phone to send out thousands of illicit text messages.

One SMS attack has been discovered that solicits a "click" and then steals money from the accounts of devices owners. Smartphone users should avoid clicking on a hyperlink that is unfamiliar and only install apps from a legitimate source.

Downloading Apps from Nefarious 3rd Parties or Other Untrustworthy Sources – An unsuspecting user can unwillingly aide and abet the delivery of malware to a device by simply downloading what appears to be a desirable app from a hacker's website. This type of threat is quite common.

Users should do all that they can to verify the authenticity of applications or programs they plan to download. Crackers and other nefarious users have hidden malware in apps that exploit private information resources.

Accidentally giving cybercriminals command and control over a smartphone can be the cause of major difficulties, such as making unauthorized charges against banks and on-line stores in which you routinely shop.

Overlay Attacks – A major threat to smartphones is the ability of crackers to hide malware underneath what appears to be a legitimate display. Underneath the genuine display could be malware waiting to be launched when the user clicks on the screen. A Trojan horse can be downloaded onto your operating system platform. One such attack vector reportedly makes it possible to turn on the video camera and microphone of computers, laptops and mobile devices.

One security publication recommends that you disable your smartphone's ability to use "scripting" and "frames". These capabilities help enable overlay attacks.

The number of overlay attacks is staggering and continues to grow. People can find hundreds of inexpensive malware tools being sold on the "dark web".

Public Charging Stations – People who use mobile computing devices often find themselves in need of charging. Using public charging stations can be a major threat. Do you use them? You should be aware that public stations where you can recharge your battery can exchange information with a mobile device when used. The attack vector is based upon the exchange of data through USB ports.

Think of your mobile computer and your smartphone, in particular, as an Internet terminal. Your smartphone is just as exposed to the threats coming from the Internet as your desktop computer.

Unless you are using a well-known and trusted re-charging station (private) you should wait until you are more certain that it is secure.

Remote Access Tools (RATs)

By definition remote access tools relate to connecting your device to another at a distance. RAT software allows for direct control of other computers and systems. Network administrators and support staff can make legitimate changes on a corporate network or personal computer. The same software, however, can be used illegitimately. That could be disastrous.

Attacks, based on RATs, may be delivered by Trojan malware.

One of the strongest defenses against threats using RATs might be the routine use of a VPN "tunnel" through which data is passed. Cracking a VPN would be, as pointed out earlier, much more difficult to accomplish.

Another defense against RAT attacks would be to use strong authentication methods.

Adware - This class of software is a menace. Just the delivery of unwanted ads to your platforms can be a genuine intrusion on your privacy. The worst adware monitors your activities and continually reports it back to the people who installed it upon your hardware.

Even major and legitimate telecommunication companies use adware to monitor the activities on the device. One threat vector, for example, is known as Carrier IQ. It's very intrusive and can be used by cybercriminals. You can learn more about Carrier IQ and its capabilities by using a search engine such as Google.

Advanced Persistent Threats (APT) – An advanced persistent threat is a class of malware that somehow has "burrowed" into a computing device and remains covert and undiscovered. For example, a user might have a device that has been compromised and each time the device is used its activities are recorded and sent back to cyber criminal(s) who are exploiting the information.

The embedded malware, once activated, goes to work and continues to function until it is discovered and removed.

Spyware – This class of software, if installed on an individual's device, can track his or her every on-line move. The word, "spyware", is a general term given to software that monitors and records your actions or keystrokes without your knowledge. A considerable amount of variety is used by malicious cybercriminals to steal or gather information.

Some companies have been known to use spyware to gather data on their customers. Most customers feel this type of monitoring is a violation of privacy, yet spyware is continually used.

Even the physical location of the mobile device's owner can be reported to the cyber criminal. A person who wishes to harass another and maintain complete "tabs" on a target's every move can do so. The cyber criminal only has to watch whatever is being done.

One of the more bizarre and recent spyware discoveries uses the smartphone's hardware microphone to listen to ultrasonic sounds being transmitted in ads to report your activities back to advertisers. Technically there is little difference between monitoring ultrasonic sounds or real speech in conversations.

One major news network reported that millions of smartphones arrive to customers with spyware already installed upon them. You should consider your phone totally compromised if it is found to have spyware installed upon it.

Trojans – This class of malware covers a multitude of threats. Generally, Trojans are installed on a device with the user's permission. People typically "click" on interesting links and eagerly download free products (e.g. possibly free ring-tone, etc.).

Upon clicking, the user unknowingly downloads malware on his or her mobile device. The malware is then activated and can result in a serious loss of confidential information. Cybercriminals can and do gain control over privately owned mobile devices. Malware can drain the battery or "jailbreak" your mobile device and elevate access privileges to gain total control. Malicious crackers can make unauthorized purchases using information stored on your hardware platform or lie in wait to be linked into a company network. The list of possible exploits is truly endless.

Insiders – You should always avoid sharing your mobile device with another individual. If you are in a corporate or business setting, the organization should have security policies that must be followed in order to protect assets.

Your personal mobile device (or company-owner device) should always remain in your possession. Cybercriminals should face multiple barriers. Giving your mobile device to another person or leaving the device unattended is simply asking for trouble. The resulting loss of critical information (whether intentional or innocent) can be significant.

Device Specific Threats – One threat associated with the iOS is referred to as Trident or Pegasus. When executed in a particular sequence, the malware results in the hacker gaining control of the iOS device. Customized versions of this iOS malware can sell for millions of dollars. Reportedly this specific malware can be very persistent and tends to focus on large companies with extremely valuable information. Researchers claim that the Trident malware can replace itself even if the phone has been patched. High value targets, when compromised, can have serious losses of sensitive data.

Connecting to Cell Phone Towers and WiFi in Foreign Countries – An individual is at risk when utilizing WiFi or cell towers in a foreign country. Most nations are without the rule of law that the U.S. has when it comes to information privacy. A nation that monitors all electronic signals, such as the People's Republic of China, has little regard for private communications unless it relates to its own state secrets.

Official government eavesdropping on electronic communications is routine in some countries. Business travelers and others should presume that there is a need for extreme caution. Your data should be encrypted and using anything less than a VPN to communicate on a mobile device would qualify as being extremely careless. Very little, if any, confidential information should be stored in a mobile device, tablet or laptop that is being taken into a foreign nation.

Vulnerabilities

A vulnerability, within the context of information security, is a weakness that can be exploited by crackers. Any list of vulnerabilities would be broad and deep. Leaving your mobile device in an unlocked car is a weakness. Failing to install a software patch from the manufacturer in a timely manner is also a vulnerability.

One report states that nearly a fourth (24.7 %) of the mobile apps that exist have at least one serious security weakness. Nearly forty percent (40%) of smartphone communications, for example, occur over unencrypted smartphones. Forty-three percent (43%) of smartphone users, however, fail to even use passcodes on their system. Consider how vulnerable your confidential information would be when transmitting it over public airways.

A research study by NowSecure discovered that more than half of mobile devices connect to insecure Wi-Fi networks on a daily basis. That's an incredible number. The pathways available to cybercriminals to access digital assets are vast.

Listed below are a number of known vulnerabilities.

1. Each mobile smartphone has a unique identifier (IMEI number) as do all computing devices (MAC addresses). Both can be revealed to crackers if the user allows their disclosure. Steps should be taken to protect the identifiers.

2. The largest user-base of smartphone operating systems is the Android. It's an unfortunate fact, however, that the Android operating system hosts the largest number of threats against it and has the most vulnerabilities. Publishers of apps for the Android, at the present time, lack the same quality control regimes

as the iOS operating system. An extremely high percentage of Android apps for sale have been hacked. Android apps generally lack the capability of having and deploying security certificates and aren't presently vetted by technical means. That fact may change in the future.

3. Smartphones, when they are connected to an infected computer for data retrieval or any type of synchronization activity, can create a two-way vulnerability because the mobile device trusts the computer and the reverse is likely true. The number of vulnerabilities becomes even more extensive when an employee synchronizes his or her smartphone with a home-based computer.

4. Any unpatched apps and security updates that the user has failed to install automatically create known vulnerabilities to known threats. Crackers constantly scan your computer, laptop and other mobile devices looking for openings to exploit. When an opening is discovered by a cybercriminal it is exploited.

5. Mobile computing offers a broad **attack surface**. For example, if you operate your mobile device with what is known as a "discovery" setting, nearby crackers would be a threat as they scan your device without your knowledge. Avoid working in a "promiscuous mode". Failing to shut down unneeded services, such as Bluetooth, would be a vulnerability.

6. Use best practices when operating your mobile devices. Follow your company's information security policies. Volunteer to serve on a committee to develop such policies if your organization is without them. Organizations without security policies have many more vulnerabilities than those with security policies.

7. Storing confidential information on your mobile device is a major vulnerability.

8. Another vulnerability associated with mobile platforms relates to blindly trusting vendors, customers, employees, fellow employees, friends and family.

9. Defective or improperly configured hardware can be a vulnerability.

10. A lack of awareness is a vulnerability. One report indicates that only eleven percent (11%) of employees with mobile devices use security best practices with their devices. A **TechTarget** survey of IT professionals reports a full spectrum of vulnerabilities come into existence when mobile devices are deployed to workers.

11. One publisher of security software reports that eighty-two percent (82%) of Android devices were found to be vulnerable when tested and to contain at least one of the twenty-five percent (25%) known operating system flaws. Hundreds of individual apps, also, were reported to contain vulnerabilities.

    Publishers emphasize that it's a slow process from the time a vulnerability is discovered to when a "patch" can be created, tested and uploaded to a user's hardware.

12. A broad range of vulnerabilities are associated with the following components: user names, IMEI identification, email, and contact information, passwords, the physical location of computing devices, and network information to which the mobile device connects.

13. Many apps, by default, can share information with other apps. This fact represents a major vulnerability that can include root access to the device.

You can get a better understanding of Android vulnerabilities by visiting the following site: http://androidvulnerabilities.org

Another source associated with Android smartphones can be accessed to keep up with security issues: https://source.android.com/security/overview/updates-resources.html

Security Measures You Can Take to Strengthen the Security of Your Mobile Devices

1.) Install legitimate updates to your operating system and apps

The publishers and manufacturers of hardware platforms, operating systems and apps frequently issue updates when vulnerabilities are discovered. Cybercriminals, specifically, create malware to exploit vulnerabilities and intrude upon your information resources. Cybercriminals tend to work at a pace that is faster than software publishers and hardware manufacturers can react.

One of the best defenses users have against cybercriminals is to quickly install updates for your mobile devices. Failing to do so guarantees a successful attack against your exposed mobile devices.

2.) Back-up the contents of your smartphone or mobile computing devices

More and more critical information is being stored on mobile devices. The loss, theft and alteration of confidential personal information is potentially catastrophic. Such data should be backed-up or the user runs a serious risk. Data can be stored in the cloud or by using other means and should only be transmitted using a secure connection like SSH or VPN.

3.) Use a complex password or phrase to log onto your mobile device

A mobile computing platform's first-line of defense is a strong and complex password. Passwords or pass phrases need to be at least eleven characters in length and ideally contain at least one special character and number. You should avoid using words that can be found in the dictionary. Constructing and using a complex password makes the task of "cracking" into a system much more difficult. Passwords or phrases should also be changed frequently.

4.) Erase sensitive and confidential data from your mobile device before re-cycling or selling it

We tend to use our technology devices for a short time. Frequently we discard older devices in an unsafe manner by simply erasing what we throw away, donate or recycle. Doing so isn't good enough to protect any confidential data stored on them.

Devices should be thoroughly erased or destroyed. There are only two methods of doing so for sure. One is to **degauss** hardware using a strong magnetic field. The other is to "shred" the hardware storage media into small fragments by using a specially designed machine that do so.

5.) Avoid downloading apps from unknown sites

Users are continuously tempted to "click" on an icon that promises desirable downloads. Cybercriminals frequently lure innocent users into downloading malware. Invitations to receive free ring tones, for example, can arrive containing malware such as what is known as "Trojans". Once such software is downloaded upon a user's device, the negative consequences can be significant. Cybercriminals can take over a device and steal sensitive personal information.

Only download software or apps from reputable sources.

6.) Encrypt all electronic communications on portable devices

Failing to encrypt the data on your portable devices leaves sensitive information exposed to cybercriminals if the device is lost or stolen. Users must also be concerned about critical information being intercepted by renegade hardware. Unencrypted information is transmitted by radio waves in plain text and easily accessed in public places.

7.) Only purchase mobile devices from reputable sources

Only purchase your smartphones and laptops from reputable sources. Cybercriminals and others have been known to sell "**jail breaked**" devices that could contain significant malware or multiple vulnerabilities. Smartphones, tablets and laptops that have had their manufacturer defaults over-ridden are likely to be open to intrusions. Significant data breaches can occur 24/7. Malware on jail breaked devices can easily be downloaded from an infected mobile phone or any computer network with which you connect.

8.) Avoid using public WiFi sites and be suspicious of using computing devices in public

Using public WiFi spots is inherently dangerous and puts your data at risk. A wireless "hot spot" is a target-rich environment for cybercriminals. In addition, you could be observed entering your password or other critical information might be read from your screen or your keystrokes. Some optical equipment and cameras can be used to assist cybercriminals.

9.) Use a Virtual Private Network (VPN)

A VPN encrypts digital data by specially packing it. Once a VPN connection is established the data that is sent from your device is encrypted, making it unreadable. When it arrives at its destination it must be "unpackaged" or decrypted. Cracking VPN communications is very difficult and resource intensive.

Many companies own and operate their own VPN. Individuals can purchase a VPN service.

10.) Enable the "device location" on your mobile device

Review how your electronic device is configured. Consider whether you want your location to be revealed to others. You, on the other hand, would have a vested interest in locating your smart phone if you misplace or leave it.

You might also want to erase the device completely and remotely if your equipment has ben lost or stolen.

11.) Avoid responding to any unsolicited messages or email from unknown senders

Cybercriminals are masters at laying traps and tricking users into clicking on their links. One such attack vectors is known as phishing. Users are presented with clever and enticing reasons as to why they should "click" on a link. Users should consider any request for "click" as being a threat and most likely an attempt to get you to download malware on your device. Digital thieves are very good at carrying out attacks known as "social engineering".

One method, discussed earlier, is an overlay attack. An unsolicited message from your bank should be viewed with extreme caution. Avoid responding. Instead, place a telephone call and ask if the bank has actually contacted you.

12.) Avoid clicking on unknown links

Frequently, our family and friends send us links to sites that claim there is an interesting story or free software to download or a variety of other reasons. You may notice a link that looks interesting but you may fail to recognize it. You must make sure that you can trust the link. Think twice before you click on any link that is unfamiliar to you.

13.) Avoid downloading apps from unknown sources (e.g. ring tones)

The apps that you download and install upon your device should be vetted. Apps for the Apple iPhone, for example, must meet the standards of the manufacturer before they can appear on iTunes. A similar mechanism for the Android platform is Google Play. You should assess each service as to the level of its robustness.

Users should be extremely careful, regardless, of downloading applications just because they sound good or are interesting. The software that you download should have good reviews and originate from responsible sources.

A detailed treatment of screening for mobile devices can be found at the link shown below:
http://nvlpubs.nist.gov/nistpubs/SpecialPublications/NIST.SP.800-163.pdf

14.) Disable Bluetooth and network discover features

Security experts recommend disabling or turning off services that aren't being used.

One service happens to be a wireless protocol known as Bluetooth. It essentially functions in a "discover mode" and seeks out connections with other Bluetooth enabled devices, such as smartphones, tablets and more.

Mobile device users need to be aware of the vulnerabilities of having Bluetooth devices operating in an always "on" condition or broadcasting your device's identity. Nefarious eavesdroppers can lock-in on your Bluetooth signal with special equipment if you are within range. You would likely be unaware.

Your contacts list on your device can be discovered. Your messages can be read and crackers can gain control.

Many people use their portable devices in discovery mode. The practice is okay as long as you need to be connected with near field communications like Bluetooth. However, you must be sure that you have taken robust security measures and disable the service when it isn't being used.

A good link related to Bluetooth and security can be found at the following link: https://www.webroot.com/us/en/business/resources/articles/corporate-security/a-review-of-bluetooth-attacks-and-how-to-secure-mobile-workforce-devices

15.) Carefully examine any "Terms of Services" that are associated with your hardware, apps or software

Most users fail to "read the fine print" associated with their hardware and software prior to beginning to use it. People are often too quick to click on the box labeled "I agree" without being aware to what they have agreed. You might be allowing the software publishers to install intrusive software on your smartphone or mobile computer. Adware is one example of software that allows publishers or manufacturers to monitor your activities.

16.) Enable encryption and use WPA2 or better

Encryption converts plain data into a form that prevents any potential intruder from reading it. Ideally, all data should be encrypted. Different platforms have various methods of scrambling confidential information that is stored or being transmitted.

Use the information at the following link to determine how to encrypt data on an Android operating system: http://www.zdnet.com/article/how-to-encrypt-your-android-smartphone-or-tablet/

17.) Use "https" when exchanging sensitive information on the web

When using the web to access or send sensitive communications make sure that "https" designation is displayed in the browser's dialog box. The "s" designation, following the letters "http", indicates that the web communications are locked down by transport layer security or SSH. It is a more secure manner of communicating on the Internet that involves authentication and certificate authorities (CAs) which is a much stronger level of security.

The following website would help the reader to better understand the concept of "https":

https://www.instantssl.com/ssl-certificate-products/https.html

18.) Safely dispose of your smartphone's SIM cards when they are going to be discarded

Smartphones contain SIM cards. The abbreviation, "SIM", stands for "Subscriber Identity Module." You might recall having to install a SIM card in your phone when you purchased it. A SIM card contains some confidential information. Your SIM card is involved in authenticating you to other devices and services.

Discarded SIMs should be destroyed. Cybercriminals who gain access to your SIM would be able to glean extremely sensitive information. The following link provides the reader with some background information:

http://www.wisegeek.com/what-is-a-sim-card.htm

19.) Set the "lock screen" function of your OS to the shortest time span as practical for you

Each mobile device's operating system has a way of "timing out" the display of the screen when the devices isn't being used. Review your product's manual to learn how to modify the length of time that your screen is displayed.

The main reason for shutting down your default display (as soon as practical) is to protect sensitive information. Any open application you are using has already "cleared" the first level of security and can be seen, read and more easily accessed or stolen. When you get up from your table in a cyber café, for example, your information is vulnerable.

20.) Avoid jail breaking your phone

Most smartphones arrive with default settings that minimize vulnerabilities. Hardware manufacturers even put limitations on their systems to prevent unauthorized software or apps from being installed and possibly granting "root access" to intruders who get into your system.

A "jail breaked" device is without the protections associated with developer vetting and may make your system vulnerable to dangerous malware being installed onto your system.

The perceived advantages to jail breaking a device is associated with the user's desire to gain more freedom over what is done with the hardware. Jail breaking your smartphone or other device, however, could render your smartphone or tablet useless.

21.) Avoid storing critical information on your mobile device

Sensitive and confidential data shouldn't be saved on your mobile devices. The danger of the equipment being stolen or "hacked" is far too great. Smart phones and tablets are normally used outside of any security perimeter. You want to avoid increasing the danger of losing your critical information.

When you must store and use sensitive information you are strongly advised to review your manual's section on how to encrypt data. Various versions of hardware and software programs have different methods and capabilities of rendering your data unusable. Encrypt all confidential files if you must have them on your tablet or smartphone.

22.) Protect devices from thieves who are in close proximity to you

Security experts will confirm that cyber thieves are always scanning for opportunities (vulnerabilities) to exploit. So should you. You would truly be better off to avoid using mobile devices in full public view. Cybercriminals shoulder surf. It is possible for a well-practiced cybercriminal to observe you entering your password.

Security experts recently estimated that more than 12,000 mobile computing devices are stolen each week. The simple act of getting up to get a napkin in a cyber café, for example, might be enough time for a cyber thief sitting next to you to make off with your mobile device.

Maintain situational awareness of your surroundings.

23.) Consider equipping your mobile device with an alarm

There are a number of devices that will sound an audile alarm if a mobile device is subjected to tampering or physically moved. You might want to consider using such a mechanism. If you are carrying a tablet or laptop, you may want to lock it inside a bag that has an alarm installed on a cable.

Avoid stepping away from your device when it's charging. Systems are now being deployed that provide lockers in public places for the safe charging of mobile devices.

24.) Avoid using AutoFill of browsers, apps and other software

The autofill functions of browsers make being on the Internet convenient. Users can have their repetitive information stored on the hardware and entered easily. However, most people are unaware that it's relatively easy for a cybercriminal to access the code that is used to display a web page and gain access to usernames, passwords and other confidential data.

Autocomplete or auto-fill is particularly risky if you authorize its use when entering passwords, PINs or security codes. Using autofill makes it easier for a cyber thief to have access to your confidential data.

25.) Log-out of apps when you have finished working upon them

You should close an application when you have completed using it. Failing to close apps, into which you are properly authenticated can leave you extremely vulnerable. At the very least, it broadens your device's attack surface, consumes memory and runs down your battery. Apps frequently enable vulnerable services (e.g. Bluetooth, etc.) that keep running.

Leaving an app "on" is a vulnerability. It is particularly dangerous if you fail to use a password on your device. You should get into the habit of logging out of sensitive apps such as shopping or bank accounts. When you exit apps that aren't being used, you are, in effect, locking a "digital back door".

Many people leave apps open for convenience sake. One source even recommends powering down your mobile platforms completely. Apps may have, also, stored data throughout your device that can cause performance problems unless the device is shut down.

26.) Turn off cookie options in your device's browser

Cookies are text files that contain ID information. They are written on your devices by websites you visit. Users are generally unaware that cookies are being written to their hardware platform to be read at a later date. The amount and type of information stored in the cookie text file varies from site to site.

Amazon's™ website uses cookies. Have you ever noticed that Amazon™ always seems to "know" what book or product you might be likely to purchase? The cookies stored on your device are matched with Amazon™'s records of your surfing and purchasing habits while on its site.

One argument for using cookies is that the practice enriches the user's experience on a company's website. People who disagree feel that using cookies reveals too much information.

27.) Be aware of social engineering (e.g. donating money to a cause in the news)

Illegitimate fund raising causes or fraudulent websites attempt to lure-in unsuspecting users. The practice is known as "social engineering". The variety of attack vectors is noteworthy.

One example of a dishonest site might be one that claims to be collecting money for the victims of a disaster that is in the news, when indeed its fraudulent. In addition to stealing your money the site might collect additional information that you willingly relinquish. Your confidential information (the credit card number you use to make a donation) can be sold to others.

Make sure you are dealing with a legitimate website when you give private information online.

28.) Be aware of the security features on your mobile device (e.g. such as being able to support certificates)

You should always enable the highest level of security provided by your brand of mobile device and its installed operating system. One strong security measure is to accept and enable certificates if possible. They assure a high-level of encryption and verify the legitimacy of the site that you are using.

29.) Use fingerprint authentication if your phone has the capability

A number of mobile computing devices now support biometric authentication such as fingerprints. Determine if this is true of your smartphone, tablet or portable computer. If so, use it.

Consider using multi-factor authentication. That might include using both a password and fingerprint recognition. Doing so would make it much more complex for cybercriminals to crack into your mobile computing device.

30.) Carefully consider security risks when enabling location services on your mobile device

Nearly all smartphone and mobile devices are capable of sharing your physical location. A significant number of software and apps request permission to use your location. You must decide if you want to add-on the potential security risks.

Little doubt exists that your privacy is reduced when you enable location services on your mobile platform. Individuals who are at risk of being stalked would want to avoid enabling an operating system or app that freely publishes your physical location to others. Some are even "always on".

Apps that use location services can contain significant bugs and make you personally more vulnerable. Location services can be very intrusive. One app was used in a third world country by an oppressive government to carry out political arrests using "location services".

31.) Notify your telecommunications provider and police immediately if you lose your phone

Internet Service Providers, or ISPs, as well as smartphone carriers, should be notified immediately if your smartphone or other digital mobile hardware is lost or stolen. Doing so can help you track down and possibly recover your lost equipment.

Most carriers have an app that can help you with recovering your phone. You should be certain that it is installed. You could possibly lock your phone with a "carriers app" and erase your data remotely after backing it up to the cloud if it's possible. You should also change your password.

32.) Use a SIM password if possible

A SIM (Subscriber Identity Module) is a plastic encased integrated circuit that is inserted into a smartphone. The SIM contains a smartphone number, an identification number and other unique data that is related to the user to whom the SIM is registered.

A SIM also has a small amount of memory that can store information, (e.g. up to 250 contacts), some SMS messages and other data used by the carrier who supplied the card. Theoretically, a SIM can be removed from one smartphone of the same type and put into another. Most SIMs that contain contact information can maintain that information and switch devices without losing their contacts data, having to change their phone number or start a new mobile contract list.

Smartphone users might want to consider using a SIM password so that no one, other than the owner, can use the smartphone's network.

33.) Avoid installing apps that ask for expanded permissions

People who use mobile computing devices (smartphones included) should be thoroughly familiar with the apps that they download and install onto their platforms. The apps or software applications should come from reputable sources and their capabilities should be understood.

Users should be careful, however, as to what permissions they grant by putting the app on their smartphone. Malicious apps might very well ask for expanded permissions. Users might easily fall for a ruse and click on "Ok". Doing so could grant the app publisher a level of permissions that can launch major security threats.

34.) Delete Apps that you don't use anymore

Apps that you don't use anymore should be deleted. Many of them could actually be running in the background taking up memory each and every time you power-up your hardware.

Another security issue is that fact that many older apps haven't been maintained or updated and may very well be "wide-open". When a Trojan or other form of malware intrudes upon confidential information on a digital device it scans for vulnerabilities. It's likely to find that unused legacy apps can reveal any number of vulnerabilities waiting to be exploited.

35.) Turn off WiFi when not in use

Security experts recommend disabling or turning off any service that isn't being used. WiFi is one such service. It also broadcasts your **SSID** over radio waves seeking out connections unless you disable it or provide other security measures to protect your information assets (such as a VPN). Crackers and cybercriminals constantly scan public WiFi sites, looking for unsecured mobile devices.

Your contacts list can be discovered. Your messages can be read and crackers can gain control over your device.

36.) Avoid posting personal information on social media sites

Many people use their smartphones and mobile devices to participate in social media.

Cybercriminals and other lawless individuals prowl social media looking for individuals whose confidential information can be stolen or *leveraged*. The list of threats is quite long. They range from stalkers gaining information on your physical location to burglars learning you are away from home and planning a break-in.

Other information that can be gleaned are the names of your children, other family members, address, birthdates, employer and any other facts about you and your habits. Limit the amount of information that you openly share.

37.) Be on guard against the capabilities of all apps

You need to be aware of what your apps are actually doing in the background. Some stay on all of the time. Others gather information on your web surfing habits and "phone home". Software that is installed on your device can access and monitor your activities and implement malware like a key logging program that records your data entry and sends it to cybercriminals.

Some apps can access data that is stored on your mobile device. Malicious software can lie in wait and monitor authentication information that you might transmit during on-line shopping, etc. This type of infor-mation can be exfiltrated (or sent) by cybercriminals.

38.) Use separate passwords on each of the apps, if possible

There are thousands of apps. Many of them have features that can re-quire the use of a PIN and keep them locked until a password or PIN is entered (multi-level authentication). Security experts would recommend that you use, if you have a choice, apps that can be locked.

If you require a PIN or password to open your device as well as an application password you are employing what is known as "two-factor authentication" to protect your information. This technique is a security best practice.

The company Google™ offers a function that allows for users to create a 16 character application password. Microsoft also offers a form of two-factor authentication.

You can find instructions on how to add multi-factor authentication by conducting an on-line search.

39.) Enable or install an app that provides for remote wiping of your phone

Security professionals recommend that you enable the remote wipe fea-ture of your mobile platforms. The primary reason is that the number of smartphones and tablets that are stolen is huge, thousands per day.

A remote wipe allows the user to access his or her digital equipment re-motely and to erase or "wipe" the data clean. Become familiar with how to enable remote wipe on your smartphone or other electronic device.

40.) Lock apps separately

A number of apps are without the capability of requiring a password to activate. There are third-party apps that can be acquired to require a password.

Conduct an on-line search for "app lockers". Include the name of your hardware platform's operating system in your search (e.g. Android, iOS). Look for responsible product reviews and select from among the best.

Be very suspicious of any **free** app lockers that are being offered. Consider calling your device's manufacturer and asking which they would recommend.

Legitimate app locker programs allow for complex passwords for numerous apps.

41.) Avoid transacting business on any public WiFi

Public wireless access points represent a target rich environment for cybercriminals. Mobile users should avoid working upon sensitive and confidential information on public WiFi sites. Avoid using any device that has been jail broken. Any and all patches should be on the smartphone.

Be mindful of your surroundings and assume that your communications are vulnerable. Be sure that all data and transactions are encrypted.

One threat that can be launched from within a public WiFi site, for example, is a Man-in-the-Middle attack. A malicious cracker can hijack a communications session between users and steal sensitive information. Attackers can establish a rogue WiFi site onto which unsuspecting users can join and be compromised.

42.) Avoid using public charging stations which can ex-filtrate information from your portable device

Public charging stations have been shown to be a potential threat. Unsuspecting users, plugging in their devices for a charge, can be compromised by malware being downloaded on their device. Data can be stolen, contact lists and confidential information can be exfiltrated and stolen.

Security experts strongly agree that you should use your own charging equipment and, if possible, use simple electrical outlets to re-charge your devices.

43.) Use a personal firewall on notebooks, laptops, tablets and other mobile devices

A firewall can be used to prevent or block access to or from a computing device. Using a firewall can significantly enhance information security.

Firewalls can either be hardware or software based. You should use one or possibly even both (depending on circumstances). Consult with your device's owner's manual to determine what firewalls are recommended.

For example, the manufacturer maintains that iOS (e.g. iPhone and iPad) is without the need for a firewall. Yet there are firewall applications that claim to be for the Apple hardware systems.

The issue of whether to use a firewall is somewhat clearer in the case of the Android operating system. Currently it can make good use of a firewall.

The best plan might be to contact the manufacturer's device support team and ask if they would recommend the use of a firewall and specifically which one(s).

44.) Consider using an application that allows you to create a more complex password

The more complex you can make passwords the better. Applications exist that can assist you in creating robust passwords. Passwords can be modified, extended and managed.

A simple on-line search for 'password generating apps' will produce a list of applications that will assist you in the process. The matter is worthy of the time that you put into learning about using a password app.

Consider asking your device's manufacturer or software publisher for recommendations. Be aware of any software that is FREE.

45.) Carry your smartphone or tablet in an inconspicuous manner and possibly lock your device

You must assume that if you are in public with your hardware, cyber-criminals are observing you and looking for vulnerability. Carry your equipment so that it won't be in view. Use a briefcase or large tote bag to conceal your tablet. Carry your smartphone in a case or in your pocket.

You can use your smartphone or tablet's locator service if you have enabled it.

46.) Label your mobile devices with selected contact information in the event that a lost device is found

Putting some type of label on your device (limited contact information) would be wise in the event that it is lost. Affix or inscribe enough information on your device so that it will be possible to recover. Leave out any personal information. Use an alternate phone number or create an email address to receive a message related to the phone's return.

47.) Look for the "padlock" icon in the browser's address bar

When a padlock is displayed in the space where you enter a website's address, it indicates that you are connected to a website that is secure. Make certain the padlock is present when you want a secure connection. There are a number of issues associated with working on secure websites.

Remember, however, that the appearance of a 'padlock' doesn't necessarily mean that the owners of the website are honest people and they could still download malware to your device.

The link below addresses a number of issues relative to communicating using secure websites:

https://www.tunetheweb.com/blog/what-does-the-green-padlock-really-mean/

48.) Install the most robust mobile security software that is available

You are aware that smartphones and tablets have different operating systems. The relative strength of numerous hardware platforms vary (iOS and Android). The largest number of threats and vulnerabilities that exist are associated with the Android operating system. The iOS (iPhone) and Windows-based tablet operating systems tend to be more secure out-of-the-box. The landscape, however, is fluid and can change (e.g. is Microsoft™ is rumored to be creating a Surface phone).0

You should investigate the security software market to learn which are the strongest security choices for your platform. Check with your hardware manufacturer and ask which security apps or software they recommend.

Consider using a VPN and software that allows you to use multi-factored authentication (i.e. more than one password or PIN).

Install software that blocks malware (e.g. Trojans).

You would, also, be interested in software that prevents cybercriminals from removing information from your device (e.g. Adware).

49.) Consider using gestures and passwords

A number of mobile computing devices are capable of using gestures (e.g. such as a circle with a swipe or slash through the middle). Gestures can be used with a PIN or password to authenticate or log on to your platform or an app.

Gesture-based authentication, by itself, is likely to be much more convenient. Preliminary research indicates that gesture-based 'passwords' may be less effective for now.

Using application based PINs and software (e.g. multifactor authentication) might be more effective.

If you choose to use gestures, you should still use a complex password to access, along with an application based password.

50.) Immediately change your passwords on accounts and social media in the event you lose your mobile device

You must change all of the passwords on your applications, bank account PINs and social media accounts should you lose your smartphone. Ideally, you would have followed security best practices for mobile devices and already let your service provider and law enforcement know your device or tablet is lost or stolen. Also, you would have enabled the 'find your phone' along with the remote wipe.

51.) Make sure you understand what each app does with your data

Applications that you install on your smartphone or tablets may be tracking you without your knowledge and reporting it back to advertisers who can misuse your personal information. One of the first things you should consider, when thinking about installing an "app", is to consider how the program uses your information. With whom is your data shared? More than half of installed apps give your data away.

Most reputable publishers will explain what they do with your data but it's usually written in the fine print. Be very cautious, once again, about installing free or popular apps without understanding how they operate.

52.) Avoid conducting banking transactions and making credit card purchases on a public WiFi

We have already addressed the inherent vulnerabilities with a public WiFi site; however completely avoid conducting business or working with other confidential information on a public WiFi site. There are multiple levels of threats that can be focused on you in a public access point.

53. Avoid responding to an <u>unexpected</u> on-line request from what appears to be a legitimate source (e.g. your bank or credit card company)

Always be careful when an *unforeseen* message arrives that appears to come from a legitimate website with which you are familiar (e.g. your bank or a credit card company). Call the company or bank that is contacting you and question its legitimacy. Phishing, as a threat, is quite common and surprisingly effective. Too many individuals respond to unsolicited requests and fail to recognize that the act of responding can cause malware to be downloaded on their mobile devices.

Summary

Threats against information systems are intense. Securing computer networks must be a priority.

We must, also, secure digital and mobile computing devices. Smartphones and tablets are as "smart", in many cases, as your desktop computer. They also store critical information. The need to defend your security boundary now extends to virtually everywhere. The more the capability of equipment, the more important it is that you "lock down" your information assets.

Business and industry are allowing and supporting access to company-wide information assets with mobile platforms. Everyone involved in the use of linking mobile networks across firewalls must take extra precautions. Mobile devices are becoming so powerful that it wouldn't be a mistake for you to consider a smartphone as being in the same league as a networked computer. Some mobile computing devices are even smarter.

Securing your mobile devices is an endless process of adopting security best practices. You must be an active participant in maintaining good mobile security. Threats and vulnerabilities must be identified. A *perfect* software security solution for mobile computing platforms doesn't exist.

Glossary

attack surface – the pathways through which malware can enter digital devices

cache – a temporary storage space in a computer or mobile device where current information is stored to speed up access time

certificates or CAs (C)ertificate (A)uthorities – A technical means assuring and certifiying digital encryption

degauss – the process of exposing storage media to extremely powerful magnetic fields so that data is destroyed

exfiltrated - the unauthorized removal of digital data from an electronic device

IOT – the **(I)**nternet of **(T)**hings is a phrase that refers to everyday objects that are "Internet enabled"

jail breaked – a term that refers to mobile devices that have had their manufacturer's default settings over-ridden

operating system – software that establishes a means for humans to interact with computers

ransomware - software that allows a cyber criminal to gain control over a mobile device until the victim pays to have it released

risk – the result of a threat and vulnerability intersecting

SIM – an abbreviation that stands for **(S)**ubscriber **(I)**dentity **(M)**odule

SMS – (S)hort (M)essage (S)ervice is a protocol used for sending short text messages commonly known as "texting"

SSID – a Service Set Identifier is a unique alphanumeric character set that identifies the network upon which a device is connected

ssl – an acronym that stands for (S)ecure (S)ocket (L)ayer that encrypts communication between a browser and a website

VPN – a (V)irtual (P)rivate (N)etwork is a strong encryption mechanism for communication over the Internet

vulnerability - an opening that can be exploited by a threat

9781543286168